Your Teen Apostolate:
Accepting and Sharing the Love of God

Andre Joseph Bottesi
Michele Elena Bondi

Illustrated by Andre J. Bottesi

JOSEPH KARL
PUBLISHING

ISBN: 978-1-935356-06-6

Michele's photograph © Kathy Rizzo, www.kathyrizzo.com

Cover design by Roseann Nieman, Niemanart Graphics, rlnieman@wowway.com

Book design and layout by Erin Howarth, erin@wildernessbooks.org

Our thanks to South Street Skatepark, www.southstreetskatepark.com

The Scripture quotations contained herein are from the New Revised Standard Version Bible, copyright 1989, by the Division of Christian Education of the National Council of the Churches of Christ in the U.S.A. Used by permission. All rights reserved.

To order additional copies, please contact:

Joseph Karl Publishing
P.O. Box 80371
Rochester, MI 48308

or visit
www.Godisatworkinyou.com

Library of Congress Cataloging-in-Publication

Bottesi, Andre J. (Andre Joseph), 1994-
  Your teen apostolate : accepting and sharing the love of God / Andre Joseph Bottesi, Michele Elena Bondi ; illustrated by Andre J. Bottesi.
    p. cm.
  Includes bibliographical references.
  ISBN 978-1-935356-06-6
  1. Catholic teenagers--Religious life. 2. Vocation--Catholic Church.
  3. Catholic Church--Doctrines. 4. Christian life--Catholic authors.
  I. Bondi, Michele Elena. II. Title.
  BX2355.B67 2009
  248.8'3--dc22
                                        2009045820

Printed in the United States of America.

This book is dedicated to
Jesus
and was written
for all
teenagers.

May every soul seek to
accept, return, and share
the love of God,
which is
all encompassing,
never ending,
and
can never be contained.

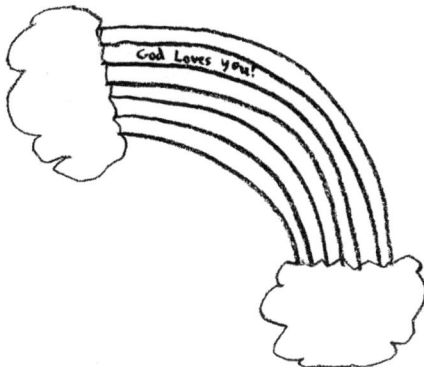

Not sure what God has in store for you?

His plans are wondrous, loving and beautiful.

Accept Him, seek Him, love Him,

and share His love with those around you.

Prepare to be amazed, for

God is at work in you!

Contents

When the Pharisees heard
that he had silenced the Sadducees,
they gathered together, and one of them,
a lawyer, asked him a question to test him.
"Teacher, which commandment in the law
is the greatest?"
He said to him,
"'You shall love the Lord your God
with all your heart,
and with all your soul, and with all your mind.'
This is the greatest and first commandment.
And a second is like it:
'You shall love your neighbor as yourself.'
On these two commandments
hang all the law and the prophets."

—Matthew 22:34-40

Foreword

Everyone wants to be loved, right? Luckily everyone is loved. Even while personally being pulled and tossed emotionally, physically, and spiritually with the experience of high school, I have been greatly comforted by knowing that I am loved by God. Sometimes, God shows it in ways you don't even expect.

God has blessed me to let me know the Bottesi family. I have shared a friendship with them for a couple years now. All the wonderful memories, from swimming at swim parks, to sledding down enormous hills in the winter, to even just seeing them every Sunday at church, has created a powerful positive influence on my life. They have always been role models, in my opinion. To me, it is pretty awesome that they can practice their faith and incorporate it into any situation.

This book, which is filled with great stories and inspirational messages, isn't just a story, it is a way of life. You will see that there are plenty of hardships in today's lifestyle. You can really begin to understand that these challenges are put there to strengthen your relationship with your best friend, God. Even if you don't realize it, there are many good things that come out of these obstacles.

For example, for three years straight, I wanted a ferret more than anything. My dad, however, was not fond of that idea. Three years of waiting, trying, and working for a chance and I always seemed to come up short. Even though it seemed hopeless and I felt horrible, I discovered that it actually held some positive points and helped shape who I am today. This experience changed my outlook on life by teaching me the importance of patience, compromise, determination, and most importantly, my faith. I prayed to God every night for an answer. Finally, after keeping my faith strong, my wish did come true and I was allowed to adopt my two pet rats as a compromise. In this book, I recognized that I wasn't alone. I found out that I had the power to get through even the toughest of times, with faith and hope.

This book, *Your Teen Apostolate: Accepting and Sharing the Love of God*, written by Michele Bondi Bottesi and her son Andre Bottesi, will take you on a journey to answer questions about yourself that you probably have never thought to ask. With personal stories and deep prayers, you too, can learn how to discover and strengthen your faith. Even just through daily experiences, like some depicted in this apostolate, you can learn to naturally incorporate our loving God throughout your day.

—Andrea Dabrowski

Introduction

Each of us has a unique personal apostolate whose genesis is God's Love. All that we are and all that we have comes from God. Thus, all that we give is an extension of His immense love. As His instruments, we must strive to be holy as we cultivate and nurture our personal apostolate and give of ourselves throughout our lives in loving service. Our efforts to accept, return, and share God's love are crucial to the formation and fulfillment of our life's work.

As St. Thérèse of Lisieux said, "God has no need for to carry out His work, I know, but just as He allows a clever gardener to raise rare and delicate plants, giving him the necessary knowledge for this while reserving to Himself the care of making them fruitful, so Jesus wills to be helped in His divine cultivation of souls."[1] God's plans are awesome

---

1 St. Thérèse of Lisieux, *Story of a Soul,* p. 113.

and wondrous, and include each one of us! May we approach our personal apostolate with tremendous excitement and great joy, relying always on His strength and guidance.

> *"Truly I tell you, just as you did it to one of the least of these who are members of my family, you did it to me."*
>
> *—Matthew 25:40*

We Are Loved

Beloved, let us love one another, because love is from God; everyone who loves is born of God and knows God. Whoever does not love does not know God, for God is love. God's love was revealed among us in this way: God sent his only Son into the world so that we might live through him. In this is love, not that we loved God but that he loved us and sent his Son to be the atoning sacrifice for our sins. Beloved, since God loved us so much, we also ought to love one another. No one has ever seen God; if we love one another, God lives in us, and his love is perfected in us.

—1 John 4: 7-12

an you remember a time when someone acted in a way that made you feel special? Perhaps you received a compliment, were thanked for something you did, or a person gave you something you wanted. How did that gesture make you feel? Maybe you felt happy, accepted, approved of, appreciated, supported, or grateful to the giver. Perhaps you felt the desire to do something nice in return.

Now think about how it feels to know that all that you are and everything you have was given to you by God. Keep in mind that everything He does comes from the great love He has for each of us. Hopefully knowing that causes you to feel happy, accepted, approved of, appreciated, supported, and grateful to God. Certainly if we recognize love shown to us by other people then we should also recognize God in every kind gesture, because He is the original source of every act of love.

You are very, very special to God. Have you ever heard the expression that God is never outdone in generosity? That is true, because all things seen and unseen come from Him. God constantly communicates with us and affirms us in many ways. He wants us all to feel loved, valued, and wanted because He loves, values, and wants us! He is the one who gave us our very first gift: the gift of life.

Just think, God created each one of us as unique individuals, out of love alone. After creating us He continually bestows His love upon us and remains with us every day throughout our lives. God demonstrates His loving presence in countless ways, communicating with us and beckoning us to have a closer relationship with Him. His method of communication varies depending on the situation. God may be profound or simple, humorous or serious. He is very symbolic and extraordinarily loving. His infinite love is reflected in everything He does! Consider just a few of the many ways each day that God demonstrates He is near you and loves you.

God communicates with us directly and also indirectly. Sometimes He speaks directly, or one-on-one. Often He communicates indirectly, through something or someone. For example, God's presence ·is revealed to us through the use of our senses in the world He created (think of the sight of a sunny beach or the taste of your favorite food). God loves us through the events in our lives, and summons us during every situation to draw closer to Him.

> One of the sweetest ways God loves us indirectly is through the actions of other people.

One of the sweetest ways God loves us indirectly is through the actions of other people. Have you ever had someone help you with your homework, or had a friend call or visit just when you needed him? Remember when someone was kind to you? That was God loving you through other people. Have you ever felt inspired to do something for someone else? That was God loving someone *through you*!

> God has loved you, loves you right now, and will always love you!

God designed a very special unit where each person is to experience the joy of being loved, valued, and wanted. That unit is the family. Every member of a family has a responsibility to express the love of God to, and receive His love from, one another. God's love for us should find its first expression from within our families. This is where each personal apostolate begins and is first shaped.

Parents and caregivers have a vital apostolate as providers of love to those God placed in their care. They have a tremendous responsibility to be faithful to their vocation as His instruments of love. Likewise, every family member is responsible for sharing and accepting the love of God. Though this may at times seem like an ordinary thing to do, being able to take part in the giving and receiving of God's love is quite extraordinary! When we love each other as God loves us, we come to see Him in one another. May we ask God often to help us with the vital work of sharing His love with those in our families.

Perhaps you received God's love from the people in your family, or from some of the people in your family. Maybe you did not receive the nurturing and love God meant for you to have from those closest to you. Rest assured that even before your family or any other person knew you, God knew you. **God has loved you, loves you right now, and will always love you!**

Sometimes accepting God's love, loving Him in return, and sharing His love with others are not easy things to do. We can be hurt by the actions of other people or by events in our lives. Sometimes our wrong choices have caused us and other people harm. Fortunately, God has the power to heal our past hurts, disappointments, and failures, and He respectfully waits for our permission to heal us, forgive us, and help us with His strength.

> Your life has great purpose, and accepting, returning, and sharing God's love are crucial to the development and fulfillment of that purpose.

When we acknowledge and accept His love, then ask for and accept His healing, God frees us so we can proceed with hope and joy. When we give God our permission, He works in us and through us. He gives us the courage and strength to forgive ourselves while constantly loving us through everything. When we place ourselves at God's service, miracles happen through our faith. We become more willing to accept love and to love in return. How beautiful!

Just by reading this book you have already started working on the best and most important relationship of your life: your relationship with God. Perhaps you started this important process already and now want make your relationship with Him even more meaningful. The contents of each chapter in this book are structured around one theme: **Your life has great purpose, and accepting, returning, and sharing God's love are crucial to the development and fulfillment of that purpose.** "If you live for Christ, not the slightest moment of your life goes to waste."[2]

This first chapter acknowledges that we are loved by God. The following chapters discuss accepting His love and loving Him in return. In conclusion, you will be challenged to become God's instrument so He can love other people through you. Hopefully God's great love for each of us will resonate on every page. Let us ask God for a greater awareness of the many ways that He loves us, invites us into a deeply personal relationship with Him, and rejoices when we love Him back.

> Fortunately, God has the power to heal our past hurts, disappointments, and failures.

---

2 Fulton J. Sheen, *Our Grounds for Hope,* p. 36

WE ARE LOVED

Celebrate What Is Right with the World

The world we live in is full of beauty. I see the beauty because I believe that God created all things. I know that beauty can be found in unexpected places. During the year I spend most of my time at school, but when I am not in school I sometimes get bored. My house is on a lot that has many trees and beautiful flowers my mom planted.

Sometimes I go outside and ignore the beauty and only focus on the negative, like the temperature, for example. If it is cold outside I focus all my attention on the cold instead of enjoying nature and all my beautiful surroundings. I need to focus on the positive, and the positive will help make my life easier and more enjoyable. Thinking positive also helps me spot more of the beauty in nature.

Sometimes I have a bad day at school. When I go home I think about the bad day I had there. Then I realize that my day actually went well. I only focused on a few negative things that happened, instead of focusing on all the numerous good things that happened. If I looked at what went well, the school day would have gone better. Focusing on the positive changes my whole mindset regarding everything I do, not just at school but at home, on vacation, and anywhere else I go. Thinking positively may help my day go even better.

This year, positive thinking will help me get through the first year of high school with dignity, good grades, and no regrets. If I think positive then maybe it will cause me to sin less. Thinking negatively may cause me to return home from school angry. That could lead me into sin. Negative thinking can cause a chain reaction. Positive thinking can also cause a chain reaction, but usually negative thinking seems to cause a bigger chain reaction! If I think of good things instead, I can return home happy and have a good day. Everything I do has a consequence, and a bad consequence is always possible.

WE ARE LOVED
Questions for You

+ Think of some ways you have received the love of God from other people.

+ What have you done for other people to make them feel loved?

+ How has God loved you directly, through your senses, or through circumstances in your life?

+ How has God loved you through other people?

+ What are some of the sweetest ways He has shown His love for you?

+What actions have you taken to love Him in return?

> Dear God,
>
> Thank You for loving me
> in so many different ways,
> directly and indirectly,
> through senses and circumstances.
> I also thank You
> for loving me
> through the people You put in my life
> to love me in Your place.
> I love You back!
>
> Amen.

2

Following The Holy Family

Now the birth of Jesus the Messiah took place in this way. When his mother Mary had been engaged to Joseph, but before they lived together, she was found to be with child from the Holy Spirit. Her husband Joseph, being a righteous man and unwilling to expose her to public disgrace, planned to dismiss her quietly. But just when he had resolved to do this, an angel of the Lord appeared to him in a dream and said, "Joseph, son of David, do not be afraid to take Mary as your wife, for the child conceived in her is from the Holy Spirit. She will bear a son, and you are to name him Jesus, for he will save his people from their sins." All this took place to fulfill what had been spoken by the Lord through the prophet: "Look, the virgin shall conceive and bear a son,

> and they shall name him Emmanuel," which means,
> "God is with us." When Joseph awoke from sleep, he did
> as the angel of the Lord commanded him; he took her
> as his wife but had no marital relations with her until
> she had borne a son; and he named him Jesus.
>
> —Matthew 1:18-25

God in His goodness never leaves us alone as we tend to our responsibilities. Not only is He always with us, He has given us wonderful role models to follow in the Holy Family. Through the examples of Jesus, Mary, and Joseph, we learn about what it means to live one's life with great love. The Holy Family experienced both the joys and hardships of life in the world. Imagine the joy Mary and Joseph felt as Jesus, the long-awaited Savior of mankind, lived among them as a member of their family! They held the infant God, Creator of the universe, as a humble baby in their arms.

The Holy Family also experienced great suffering, and how they responded to hardship is very significant. We know from Bible accounts that Jesus, Mary, and Joseph did not live a carefree life up to the time of Jesus' passion and crucifixion. They endured many hardships including poverty, pain, sorrow, relocation, threats to safety, deception, temptation, mistreatment, rejection, abandonment, fatigue, uncertainty, physical discomforts, persecution, cruelty, hostility, unfairness, and personal loss.

Like us, Jesus, Mary, and Joseph each had a personal apostolate. They agreed to be instruments of God's great love. Every person ever created is a beneficiary of the love of Jesus, Mary, and Joseph. God's plan to redeem the human race was fulfilled because the Holy Family cooperated with Him in good times and in times of suffering. Think about them when you are tempted to feel that suffering has no value! Let us consider some events from the lives of the Holy Family.

Mary showed great faith when she consented to become the Mother of Jesus (Luke 1:38). Pope Benedict XVI explained, "Mary's greatness consists in the fact that she wants to magnify God, not herself....She knows that she will only contribute

> Every person ever created is a beneficiary of the love of Jesus, Mary, and Joseph.

to the salvation of the world if, rather than carrying out her own projects, she places herself completely at the disposal of God's initiatives."[3] For his part, Joseph trusted in God even though he did not know the circumstances of Mary's pregnancy (Matthew 1:18-21). God chose that His Son Jesus be born into poverty (2 Corinthians 8:9; Luke 2:7), which meant a life of poverty for Mary and Joseph. Imagine how Joseph suffered as he tried in vain to find suitable shelter for Mary to deliver the Son of God into the world, *"because there was no place for them in the inn"* (Luke 2:7).

Mary and Joseph were obedient in presenting Jesus in the Temple in Jerusalem (Luke 2:22), where they heard the sorrowful prophecy of Simeon, *"This child is destined for*

---

3 Pope Benedict XVI, *Deus Caritas Est* ("God Is Love"), #41

the falling and the rising of many in Israel, and to be a sign that will be opposed so that the inner thoughts of many will be revealed—and a sword will pierce your own soul too" (Luke 2:34-35). At God's command, the Holy Family had to leave their home and relocate to a foreign land because Herod wanted to kill the child Jesus (Matthew 2:13-15). Later they obediently returned to Nazareth (Matthew 2:19-23). Jesus wept with sorrow at the death of His friend Lazarus (John 11:33-35) and later for the people of Jerusalem (Luke 19:41-44). During Jesus' public ministry men tried to trick Him with words (Luke 11:53-54) and also conspired against Him (Luke 20:20). Jesus was tempted by the devil (Luke 4:1-2; Luke 4:13), and betrayed by one of His Apostles for thirty pieces of silver (Matthew 26:14-16).

> May we try our best to live obedient, holy lives, through good times and bad times, even when we do not understand exactly what God has planned.

In the Garden of Gethsemane Jesus became sorrowful and troubled (Matthew 26:36-37). "He now sensed guilt to such an extent that it forced Blood from His Body, Blood which fell like crimson beads upon the olive roots of Gethsemane, making the first Rosary of Redemption."[4] *"And going a little farther, he threw himself on the ground and prayed, 'My Father, if it is possible, let this cup pass from me; yet*

---

4 Fulton J. Sheen, *The Life of Christ*, p. 321-322

not what I want but what you want.'" (Matthew 26:39). He was arrested and led away by armed soldiers and officers (Mark 14:43-46; John 18:12), forced to stand trial (Matthew 27:11-14), and sentenced to death by crucifixion (Luke 23:23-25). Imagine the sorrow of His loving Mother as she witnessed the cruelty her beloved Son took upon Himself to satisfy Divine justice. *"Then they spat in his face and struck him; and some slapped him, saying, 'Prophesy to us, you Messiah! Who is it that struck you?'"* (Matthew 26:67-68).

"And they clothed Him in a purple cloak; and after twisting some thorns into a crown, they put it on him. And they began saluting him, 'Hail, King of the Jews!' They struck his head with a reed, spat upon him, and knelt down in homage to him. After mocking him, they stripped him of the purple cloak and put his own clothes on him. Then they led him out to crucify him" (Mark 15:17-20). *"And carrying the cross by himself, he went out to what is called The Place of the Skull, which in Hebrew is called Golgotha. There they crucified him, and with him two others, one on either side, with Jesus between them"* (John 19:17-18). Jesus was rejected by many people, among them some of His closest followers (Mark 14:66-72). John was the only Apostle present at the foot of the Cross. As Jesus was being crucified soldiers divided the garments of their Savior by casting lots (Matthew 27:35). Others mocked

> May we wisely seek to imitate the love, faith, sanctity, courage, and obedience of the Holy Family.

Him (Matthew 27:39-44). **Jesus forgave everyone** (Luke 23:34).

Jesus' decision to suffer and die to redeem us is the greatest act of love mankind has ever known. His personal apostolate was one of tremendous love! We know the whole story today, but the people of Jesus' time did not know how the events of their time would play out. The members of the Holy Family were obedient even when they did not understand God's plan. They did not demand that God tell them everything in advance. They did not insist that God give them exactly what they wanted when they wanted it.

> The members of the Holy Family were obedient even when they did not understand God's plan.

Jesus, Mary, and Joseph were obedient to God and did not give up, even when doing what God asked them to do involved tremendous personal suffering. What faith, what courage! Their courage and strength came from God. May we try our best to live obedient, holy lives, through good times and bad times, even when we do not understand exactly what God has planned. May we wisely seek to imitate the love, faith, sanctity, courage, and obedience of the Holy Family.

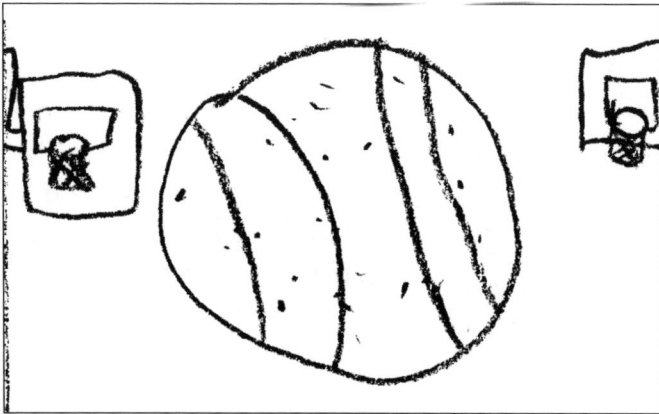

FOLLOWING THE HOLY FAMILY
Basketball and Life

When I was in 7th grade I played basketball at the YMCA. The season was four months long and divided up into two sessions. During the first session my team lost every game. We almost won one game, but a boy on the other team made a half-court shot at the final buzzer. I was upset about not winning a single game. Several of the boys on my team got frustrated and quit.

During the second part of the season my team had some new players and a different coach. That coach went through things slower and was nicer when we made mistakes. During the first game I was nervous because I was afraid that we were going to lose again. We won our first game and every single game after that. We were undefeated in the tournament and came in first place. I was excited, got a trophy, and celebrated by going out to eat with my family.

My younger brother Nick also played basketball at the YMCA and was on a team with younger boys his age. During the first session his team lost all of their games except for the three they won because the other teams did not show up. During the second session Nick's team lost all of their games except for the final one, although many of the games were very close contests. My brother was upset that he only won one game, but he and his teammates were so glad to win their last game, which went into double overtime. His team came in second to last in their tournament. Nick was gracious to me when I won my trophy, even though he really wanted to win one, too. His team's record did not reflect how well they played and I am proud of my brother's performance.

Nick and I enjoyed playing basketball at the YMCA. The coaches were balanced and did a good job of giving every-one an opportunity to play while remaining competitive. The next year we decided to play basketball for our school. The practice schedule was more demanding and the game locations were much farther away. The expense in time and money was much greater. The players on my team worked very hard but we won only one game. Most of the time my coach would not let me play. At my middle school there were some coaches that allowed all the children to play and there were some coaches that only let certain kids play. In the beginning I was so excited to play for my school. Most of the team worked hard. I always tried my best to work hard and honor the commitment that I made.

One of my games was an hour's drive away from our house. Several members of my family came to watch, and I only got to play for 93 seconds. During another game we were not even close to winning but the coach still would not let me play. He played the same few boys over and over. During another game I watched the same boys play over and over, and two other boys joined with me and pleaded with the coach from the bench to let us play. He did not listen. I felt used by not being used. I just wanted to play basketball. During practices my coach had me sit out more often than the other boys. I felt angry and frustrated. I understood it is sometimes necessary to play certain people during games, but then I should have been given more of an opportunity to practice so I could improve.

My mother and I talked to the coach but nothing changed. My mom felt my frustration and told me that God must have something for me to learn because there was no explanation for why I was treated so unfairly. One boy on my team was allowed to play two sports at the same time, be late for games and practices, yet the coach let him practice and play frequently when he was there. My mother was so proud of me for always supporting the boys on my team who got to play most of the time, including the coach's son. Those teammates did not reciprocate that to me or encourage the coach to be fair and let everyone play.

After winning a trophy last year I was hopeful of winning another one this year, but I realize that I cannot win them all. During the awards ceremony we listened as every coach made a speech. Some of the coaches talked about how often they won, but I respect the coaches who talked about playing fair, including everyone, enjoying the sport, and playing as a team. Sure, winning is fun, but some things are more important than winning at all costs. Since I was kept out of the game so often, I got to watch the game and learn more about it. I got a chance to know the boys who were also kept out. Sometimes the best player or the one who makes the winning basket is the child who really wants the opportunity to play, has a balanced approach to the game, and has the most heart.

FOLLOWING THE HOLY FAMILY
Questions for You

+ What are some of the joys you have in common with Jesus, Mary, and Joseph?

+ What are some of the hardships you have in common with those of the Holy Family?

+ What has God requested of you in your life so far, and have you responded as the Holy Family did?

+ Have you asked God to help you?

Dear Lord,

Thank you for providing
wonderful examples
for us to follow
in Jesus, Mary, and Joseph.
Please guide us and strengthen us
through joys and trials
as we seek to emulate
the Holy Family
and remain faithful to Your will.

Amen.

3

Called To Faith

Once while Jesus was standing beside the lake of Gennesaret, and the crowd was pressing in on him to hear the word of God, he saw two boats there at the shore of the lake; the fishermen had gone out of them and were washing their nets. He got into one of the boats, the one belonging to Simon, and asked him to put out a little way from the shore. Then he sat down and taught the crowds from the boat. When he had finished speaking, he said to Simon, "Put out into the deep water and let down your nets for a catch." Simon answered, "Master, we have worked all night long but have caught nothing. Yet if you say so, I will let down the nets." When they had done this, they caught so many fish that their nets were beginning *to break. So they signaled their partners in the other boat to come and help them. And they came and filled both boats, so that they began to sink. But when Simon Peter saw it, he fell down at Jesus' knees, saying, "Go away from me, Lord, for I am a sinful man!" For he and all who were with him were amazed at the catch of fish that they had taken; and so also were James and John, sons of Zebedee, who were partners with Simon. Then Jesus said to Simon, "Do not be afraid; from now on you will be catching people." When they had brought their boats to shore, they left everything and followed him.*

—Luke 5:1-11

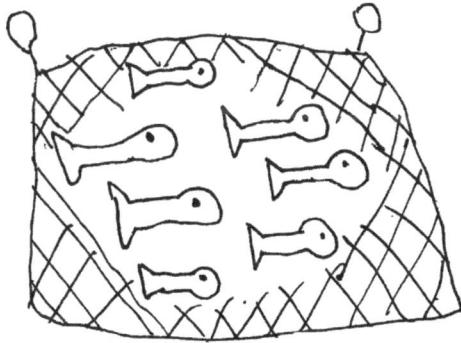

To allow one's self to be called to faith is to take a step closer to God. Having a personal relationship with God is necessary to our discipleship. We need to know God to recognize and understand what He asks of us. We need His strength and guidance. As we continue to allow ourselves to be enticed to faith, we become even closer to Him and grow in holiness. Let us consider a few of the many ways that we are drawn to faith each day. Have you ever had someone smile at you? Has someone ever helped you in any way? Then you have been called to have faith!

Have you been around another person? Or looked at yourself in a mirror? Has someone been an inspiration to you? You have been called to faith! Have you laughed lately? Have you spoken to a small child? Were you ever worried about someone else? Have you ever cared about anything? You were being called to have faith!

Have you ever seen the rays of the sun streaming through the trees on a bright morning? Do you have a favorite song? Have you ever looked at a beautiful picture? Have you ever been lost in a daydream? Can you think of a time you saw a colorful sunset or a harvest moon? Have you ever noticed the whiteness of snow, jumped in it, touched it, tasted it, shoveled it, or slid down it? You were being called to have faith!

Have you ever bounced a ball really, really high up in the air? Or jumped in a huge pile of leaves? Did you ever look at the leaves in fall and think about their Creator? Have you ever been concerned with the environment? Have you ever felt a soft breeze? Have you ever considered

> Have you ever felt grateful for something? Have you ever thanked God for anything? Have you ever heard a giggle? You were being called to have faith!

how many different flowers, animals, flavors, snowflakes, or people there are? Oh, how you were being called to have faith!

Did you ever feel happy? Have you ever said a prayer? Have you ever found holiness in a moment of silence? Have you ever wanted to visit God in His house after passing a church? You were being drawn to faith! Have you ever felt grateful for something? Have you ever thanked God for anything? Have you ever heard a giggle? You were being called to have faith!

Have you ever thought about what it is like to be loved more than you can ever imagine, forever and ever, no matter what, just because you are you? Did you ever have something sad happen that caused you to suffer, but your suffering led to something good? Were others inspired by your courage? Guess what? You became closer to God when you allowed yourself to have faith. Chances are that God has even worked through you in many ways to encourage others to have faith!

In the Bible the Gospel of Luke tells us the story about Simon and the other fishermen attempting in vain to catch fish, while Jesus drew people to faith through His teaching. Imagine Simon's reaction when Jesus joined the fishermen and requested that Simon let down the nets. The fishermen had caught nothing all night! Despite making a logical and educated guess that they would still not catch any fish, Simon allowed himself to be called to faith. He did what Jesus asked him to do.

They ended up catching so many fish that their nets were breaking! Simon had to ask the fishermen in another boat to help them with all the fish. Everyone was amazed that this time Simon caught so many fish. Simon then apologized to Jesus for his lack of faith. He said, "Go away from me, Lord, for I am a sinful man!" Have you ever found yourself in a situation like Simon's, when you were encouraged to have faith? Can you place yourself in the story in Simon's place? What would you have done?

God works with us like He did with Simon, and asks each of us to believe and trust in Him. So many times we respond with disbelief as Simon did. Sometimes we think our ideas are better than God's ideas. Sometimes we tell

> Sometimes we think our ideas are better than God's ideas. Sometimes we tell God that what He has in mind is not possible.

God that what He has in mind is not possible. Simon thought he was using good logic when he said, "Master, we have worked all night long but have caught nothing." What do you think would have happened if Simon refused to be obedient? What happens when we refuse to have faith?

> What role does God have for you in His plan of salvation? To find out, allow yourself to have faith!

Simon allowed himself to have faith in Jesus and obeyed, saying, "Yet if you say so, I will let down the nets. " Jesus then said to Simon, "Do not be afraid; from now on you will be catching people." The apostolate of Simon and the other disciples changed when they agreed to be followers of Christ. They were fishermen and became fishers of men. As a result of their obedience, God was able to use them to introduce and teach the Catholic faith to people all over the world.

By choosing to have faith, Simon and the Apostles helped God with His plan of salvation. Our obedience is pleasing to God and necessary to our Christian life. Obedience is necessary so God can work through us. He will not act in us without our permission. What role does God have for you in His plan of salvation? To find out, allow yourself to have faith!

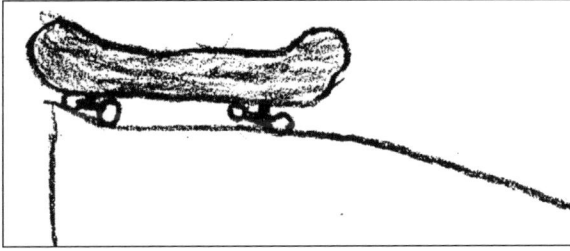

CALLED TO FAITH
Casting Out Our Nets

One day I went fishing with my dad, brother, sister, and Uncle Billy. We began fishing sometime around 11:00 a.m. First we used rubber worms to try and catch fish. We cast out into the lake and waited for about 10 to 20 minutes but did not catch anything. Then my brother Nick noticed that the dock on the other side of the lake had a "No Fishing" sign, but that was where all the big fish were. So we tried casting our lines really far out to that dock. That did not work; the dock was just too far away. Even if we were able to cast out that far we could not get a fish because we would not be able to reel the fish in fast enough and the fish would have gotten away.

Since we were not catching any fish, my dad suggested we use raw hot dogs as bait instead. He went back to the house and got them. We hooked the hot dogs and cast them out but kept losing them. The fish were either biting them off the hook or they fell off. I set my reel down, walked down the shore, and noticed that there were a lot of fish close to shore. However, they were not very big compared to what I hoped we would catch.

I then reeled my line back in and went over to the place where I saw the fish. While waiting for a nibble I noticed that all the little fish were interested in the hot dogs but the big fish were not! I noticed a really big fish a little farther out, about five feet from my line. So I reeled my line back in and threw the line out toward the big fish. I was excited and told everyone else to come over and help me catch it. I was not able to catch it because it did not want to bite, but my Uncle Billy cast out his line and caught a big one. He took a couple of pictures of the fish and then threw it back in.

I was determined to catch a really big fish like my Uncle Billy did. Every time I saw a fish I cast out my line but they never seemed to bite. I decided to stop fishing and sat in the shade for a little bit. Then I got up and asked my dad how much longer we were going to stay. He said, "Another 20 minutes." I wanted to catch something at least. Then my brother caught a fish. Nick's fish was not as big as our uncle's but the catch was still inspiring enough for me to want to catch one just like his. Nick caught his fish really close to shore. The fish that seemed so little before were actually big because the light hitting the water made the fish look smaller than they were.

I was really excited when I finally caught a fish. My fish was bigger than my brother's. We took some pictures and then threw the fish back. Nick caught another fish and then I caught another one. When we left the lake I was happy that I had caught some fish. I still enjoyed fishing even though I did not catch a fish as big as I had hoped I would. When I was not catching any fish and the hot dogs were not really working, I still believed that catching fish was possible and so I kept trying. Our time at the lake did not just involve catching fish but was also about spending time with people we care about and enjoying life as we are called to faith. We have to make sure we keep casting out our nets like the disciples did, both while fishing and in life in general. We must always have faith in God. With God, all things are possible!

CALLED TO FAITH
Questions for You

+ What are your favorite titles for Jesus?

+ Are you willing to be called to faith and allow your faith to grow?

+ In what ways have you been called to faith?

+ How have you responded?

+ How is God calling you closer to Him, and what are you doing to give Him the proper place in your life?

Dear God,

Please help us
recognize
the many ways
You attract us to faith,
for the first step
in having
a relationship with You
is recognizing Your presence.

Amen.

4

Accepting God's Love

One of the criminals who were hanged there kept deriding him and saying, "Are you not the Messiah? Save yourself and us!" But the other rebuked him, saying, "Do you not fear God, since you are under the same sentence of condemnation? And we indeed have been condemned justly, for we are getting what we deserve for our deeds, but this man has done nothing wrong." Then he said, "Jesus, remember me when you come into your kingdom." He replied, "Truly I tell you, today you will be with me in Paradise."

—Luke 23:39-43

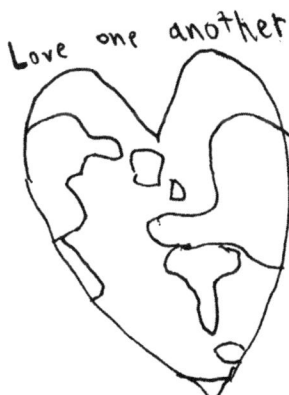
Love one another

Think of just one good friendship you have had and what that relationship has meant to you. Now imagine what a closer relationship with God will mean to you! If we want to have close relationships with people, it makes sense to first and foremost have a close relationship with the One who created us, loves us, and wants to be loved by us in return. Have you ever heard the expression "To have a friend, be a friend"? Ask yourself: Do I welcome God's presence and goodness in my life, or am I rejecting Him?

Do I even recognize God's presence? If so, how often do I accept Him? Only when things in my life are going good? Only when things are very difficult for me? Once a month? Every Sunday, perhaps at Christmas, a little during Lent and most likely at Easter because that is a Holy Day *and* a Sunday? Do you realize God is with each of us every moment of every day? How many times we are tempted to say, "Not now, God." How often we create and nurture relationships on our terms, not giving any consideration to what others want or need. How often we treat God the same way!

The first step to beginning any relationship is to make the decision to have a relationship. To have a relationship with God, we must respond to His calling by deciding that we want to have a relationship with Him. Just like relationships with people require work, so too does our relationship with God. Decision first, effort second! Healthy relationships need love, respect, effort, nurturing, time, good communication, patience, trust, understanding, forgiveness, and sacrifice from both parties.

God is the best role model there is for having happy relationships. In His relationship with us, God always gives us love, respect, attention, nurturing, and a lot of time. He communicates openly with us and is patient as we learn, make mistakes along the way, and make progress. We can always trust Him, and He is always very respectful. God never forces us to do anything, and allows us to make decisions for ourselves. As a caring Father, He also gave us rules to follow in the Ten Commandments.

> How often we create and nurture relationships on our terms, not giving any consideration to what others want or need. How often we treat God the same way!

In His relationship with us, God is infinitely and unconditionally loving and understanding. He is not distant but is always close. He is forgiving. God is also sacrificial, dwelled among us as our Brother, and opened the gates of salvation to all who will accept it. *"This is my commandment, that you love one another as I have loved you. No one has greater love than this, to lay down one's life for one's friends"* (John 15:12-13).

When we think about the time and effort we put into relation- ships, we get information

> **God is the best role model there is for having happy relationships.**

about ourselves that helps us understand the quality of our relationships. Looking at our behavior this way can lead to personal growth, make our relationships better, and can be put to good use in the work of our apostolate. Relationships suffer when they are neglected. Regardless of the current quality of our relationship with God, He always loves us, al- ways pursues us, always welcomes us, and is always willing to take up where we left off. No matter what effort we put forth, God always does His share. Let us eagerly meet our most loving God halfway.

Think of how many times you have been judged, blamed, rejected, neglected, or condemned by another person for something that you have or have not said or done. Think of how many times you have acted this way toward others. How many relationships end because of a lack of forgiveness. What pain we feel when we are judged, blamed, rejected, neglected, condemned, or not forgiven. Imagine how God feels when we judge, blame, reject, neglect, condemn, or hold a grudge toward Him. How many times we unfairly reject God! Yet He eagerly awaits our return and always welcomes us back.

The Gospel of Luke shows Jesus continually exercising His ministry of pardon.[5] Luke 23:39-43 tells us that the

---

5 *The Jerome Biblical Commentary*, p. 161

Good Thief crucified on the cross next to Jesus recognized and admitted that his own punishment was fair. In his terrible condition, the guilty man accepted responsibility for his actions. At a time that could have been one of such great despair, he allowed himself to have faith. He asked Jesus for forgiveness and accepted salvation.

> Each of us has the opportunity to have a relationship with someone who knows us better than anyone.

Why would the actions of this particular person be mentioned in the Bible? The Good Thief was compassionate to our Lord, who came to save everyone. At the moment Jesus saved the entire human race, one of the people who Jesus came to save recognized his Savior. He acknowledged Jesus as severely and unjustly punished, who instead of resisting forgave and redeemed every sinner. Imagine the joy the Good Thief's decision gave our suffering Lord! May we also give Jesus the joy of accepting His love and forgiveness.

We realize from the conversation between the thieves crucified with Jesus that the Good Thief acknowledged his Savior *and* was remorseful for his sins. "Do you not fear God, since you are under the same sentence of condemnation? And we indeed have been condemned justly, for we are getting what we deserve for our deeds, but this man has done nothing wrong." The story of the Good Thief is important because he acknowledged Jesus' personal ministry of sacrificial love and forgiveness and accepted Jesus' entire offer, all in one sentence! "Jesus, remember me when You come into Your kingdom."

Jesus responded with a loving pardon: "Truly I tell you, today you will be with Me in Paradise." For his trust, the Good Thief was rewarded and shortly thereafter joined Jesus in heaven. May we learn from what we have been taught by the personal apostolate of the Good Thief and accept the redemption offered to us by our Savior, accept responsibility for our actions, and treat everyone with the mercy shown to us by Jesus.

Each of us has the opportunity to have a relationship with someone who knows us better than anyone. God knows us even better than we know ourselves. Imagine having a relationship with someone who is always available and is always patient, kind, and merciful.

> Imagine having a relationship with someone who is always available and is always patient, kind, and merciful.

God never rejects us, always listens to us, and is always willing to reconcile with us. Envision having a close relationship with the One who loves you so immensely that He gave His life so that you could spend eternity in His most loving Presence.

Once we choose to begin a relationship with God or improve the relationship we have with Him, and truly work at it, our relationships with other people also improve. There is more peace. We are better able to carry out our apostolate and are happier. Let us model all our relationships on God's relationship with us. We can begin like the Good Thief did, by welcoming Him into our lives and accepting His love, for He comes where He is welcomed.

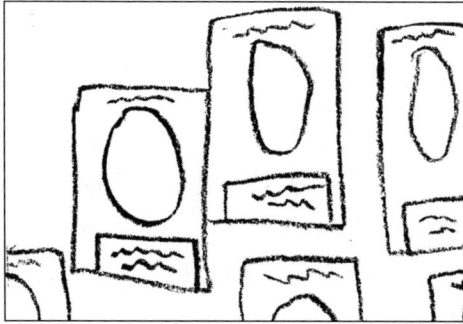

ACCEPTING GOD'S LOVE

Collecting Cards, Collecting God's Love

I like to watch my favorite shows on television. There is one show I like that is made in Japan. Collectible cards based on the show are sold at many different stores. The cards usually come in sets of nine cards per pack, but there are tins that come with five to seven packs and have one rare card displayed on the front of the tin. My collecting began when I was on a trip at the age of seven. I was watching my favorite show and then saw a commercial for their card game. I really wanted to buy some cards so the next day at a grocery store, my brother and I each bought a pack.

Back at the hotel we opened our packs and each had nine cards. We then realized that the writing on the cards was in Japanese. We were disappointed because we could not read any of the cards, including the strong card that my brother had. However, we were still happy because at that time we could not read that much anyway, and we could read the numbers and look at the pictures. The names of the cards remained a mystery to us.

I have been collecting cards for seven years and have

over 200 cards. I started out sorting the cards into three tins: the first tin contained my best cards, the second tin held my bad cards, and all the other cards were put in the third tin. I was running out of room in the tins for my cards until my brother suggested to our mom that she get me a plastic card holder and give it to me for Easter. I was really surprised and excited when I received the card holder. All my cards fit in it and are organized.

I enjoy buying new cards but always get a lot of doubles. I want to get strong cards but one never knows how many strong cards are in the packs. Every time I buy cards I get tired of them after a while and want to buy new ones. There was a certain card that I had been wanting and one day I saw it in a store. I spent my money to get it and was happy. I put the card inside a special card holder so it would not get damaged.

That card remains my favorite. Since buying that card I have not collected many other cards because I already had my favorite card and plenty of other cards. I also realize that I am never going to be able to collect every card. I know that happiness does not come from buying things but from spending time with God in church and in prayer. I enjoy using the cards I have and appreciate what I have already been given.

There are always new cards in the stores, including shinier ones. I need to keep my collecting and buying reasonable. We can always put our time and trust into God, and His love does not cost us anything. Jesus' love for us did cost Him everything, however. Sometimes we think we need to buy more things when in fact it is our relationship with God that needs our attention and that is the cause of our feeling in need of more things. When we make time to be with Him and grow close to Him, receive Him, and place ourselves at His service, then everything we have and all that we do has true value.

ACCEPTING GOD'S LOVE
Questions for You

+ How much effort do you put into the relationships that matter to you?

+ What is the quality of those relationships?

+ How much effort are you putting into your relationship with God?

+ What is the quality of your relationship with Him?

+ What have you done to welcome His presence in your life and meet Him halfway?

+ How has your relationship with God affected your discipleship?

Dear God,

Help us to recognize
Your many invitations
to have a closer relationship
with You.
Grant us the grace
to meet You halfway,
and accept
Your loving offer of
salvation and sanctification.

Amen.

5

Loving God Back

So he came to a Samaritan city called Sychar, near the plot of ground that Jacob had given to his son Joseph. Jacob's well was there, and Jesus, tired out by his journey, was sitting by the well. It was about noon. A Samaritan woman came to draw water, and Jesus said to her, "Give me a drink" (His disciples had gone to the city to buy food). The Samaritan woman said to him, "How is it that you, a Jew, ask a drink of me, a woman of Samaria?" (Jews do not share things in common with Samaritans). Jesus answered her, "If you knew the gift of God, and who it is that is saying to you, 'Give me a drink,' you would have asked him, and he would have given you living water." The woman said to him, "Sir, you have no bucket, and the well is deep. Where do you get that living water? Are you greater than our ancestor Jacob, who gave us the well, and with his sons and his flocks drank from it?" Jesus said to her, "Everyone who drinks of this water will be thirsty again, but those who drink of the water that I will give them will never be thirsty. The water that I will give will become in them a spring of water gushing up to eternal life." The woman said to him, "Sir, give me this water, so that I may never be thirsty or have to keep coming here to draw water."

—John 4:5-15

In the first four chapters of this book we recognized that God always loves us. We learned from the lives of the Holy Family and look to their example to guide us as we carry out our life's work. We considered some of the many ways we are called to faith each day and saw ourselves as instruments of God encouraging others to have faith. We discussed how accepting God's love leads us into closer relationship with Him and with others.

This chapter takes us another step closer to God as we consider returning to God the unconditional love that He gives to us. By answering the questions at the end of the first four chapters, you have already grown closer to the Love of your life. Already your efforts have led toward accepting God's love as you allow your faith to grow. Now we move on to our responsibility to love God back, for "love is repaid by love alone...."[6] Before we can love in return we must first be willing to accept love, so let us first consider how we respond to being loved.

Ask yourself these questions. How do you respond to love in general? Are you comfortable receiving love and loving in return? Do you feel worthy of being loved? How many reasons we can come up with for not being worthy of love! Many times we reject love and are not even aware that we

---

6 St. Thérèse of Lisieux, *Story of a Soul,* p. 195

are doing it. Have you ever done that? Recognizing how we respond when others express kindness, empathy, and compassion to us and understanding the reasons behind why we act that way are very important. In order to be loved we must give our permission to be loved. There is no doubt God wants us to accept His love in the many ways that He sends it.

When someone compliments you, do you accept the compliment with humble gratitude, do you hesitate to accept the gesture, or do you totally reject the compliment? How do you respond when someone offers to help you? Do you accept a helping hand, recognizing the love of God in the offer? Do you accept help only if you absolutely have to? Or do you reject help, perhaps not wanting to bother anyone?

So often we get into the habit of rejecting love. We may do this with the best of intentions. However, we reject God's love when we act this way. Rejecting the love of God through the actions of other people stops the work God is trying to accomplish through them. An awareness of how we respond to being loved

> Recognizing how we respond when others express kindness to us and understanding the reasons behind why we act that way are very important.

and understanding when and why we reject love helps us to see our responses to love in a healthier way. God never refuses our love, so let us fully accept the love that God sends to us, directly and indirectly. Then joyfully return this love to God, directly and also indirectly by sharing His love with other people. *"Truly I tell you, just as you did it to one of the least of these who are members of my family, you did it to me"* (Matthew 25:40).

> Let us fully accept the love that God sends to us, directly and indirectly.

In the story of the Samaritan woman at the well presented at the start of this chapter, Jesus was tired from traveling and went to the well to ask the woman for a drink. In her autobiography *Story of a Soul*, St. Thérèse commented on the conversation Jesus had with the woman. "See, then, all that Jesus lays claim to from us; He has no need of our works but only of our love, for the same God who declares He has no need to tell us when He is hungry did not fear to beg for a little water from the Samaritan woman. He was thirsty. But when He said: 'Give me to drink,' it was the love of His poor creature the Creator of the universe was seeking. He was thirsty for love."[7]

Accept God's love in all the many different ways He cares for you and be sure to love Him back. We accomplish this directly and through the work we do in our imitation of Christ. During the final moments of His mortal life Jesus stated from the Cross, *"I am thirsty"* (John 19:28). God thirsts for our love! "If Jesus Christ thirsted for souls, must not a Christian also thirst? Has He not called us to be His Apostles and His Ambassadors, in order that His Incarnation might be prolonged through the continued dispensation of the divine through the human?"[8] We can quench God's great thirst by loving Him back.

7 St. Thérèse of Lisieux, *Story of a Soul*, p. 189
8 Fulton J. Sheen, *The Rainbow of Sorrow*, p. 62-63

LOVING GOD BACK
Things Are Looking Up

There is a lot to be said for looking up. Synonyms for the word "up" are happy, positive, and upbeat. When we want to encourage someone, we say, "Things are looking up!" We are told to "hold our heads high" to inspire confidence. In life we can "reach new heights," "reach for the stars," are "at the height of our career." We can aspire to "set our sights higher." We "look up" to someone admirable.

Why all this looking up? My brother Nick, sister Alyssa, Mom, and our wonderful friend Alice joined me in considering why people think so highly about looking up. When we look up we see all kinds of birds, roofs, leaves, stars, lights, clouds, the blue sky, planes, and sunbeams. Look up and spot helicopters, the Northern Lights, the Air Force, rainbows, raindrops, the moon, balloons, a sunset, parachutes, rain, skyscrapers, the sun, trees, and hail. Just by tilting our heads up we can see snowflakes, sleet, leaves blowing in the wind, and seagulls at the beach.

Up above us we see kites, parasails, bungee jumpers, a

waterfall, lights, fireworks, confetti, bubbles, and adults. Lift your eyelids and see rockets launching, planets, lightning, tornadoes, canyons, mountains, dust particles floating in the air, and signs. When we raise our eyes we see houses, horses, hot air balloons, giraffes, trucks, taller folks, semis, elephants, extended fire truck ladders, and a wrecking ball.

Look up and see the beginning of something wonderful, like when caps are joyfully tossed into the air at graduations and when rice is thrown at a wedding. When you look up you can see your bangs, your mom or dad, the brim of your hat, your eyelashes, and many different kinds of ceilings. What else do **you** see when **you** look up?

When I think of looking up, I also think of God and all the magnificent things He has created and inspired us to create. I think of "looking up" to Him, for God is perfect and His plans are perfect. His love is the standard by which we should aspire to love Him and one another. Take time to look up and share a special moment with God and with those around you.

LOVING GOD BACK
Questions for You

+ How do you respond when love is shown to you by others?

+ Is it easier for you to accept love from people when realizing that all love comes from God?

+ Do you see yourself as worthy of God's love?

+ When you recognize yourself as worthy of love and understand that God wants to love you, is it easier to accept the many ways God loves you each day?

+ Is it easier then to love God, yourself, and others in return?

Dear God,

You love us
so gently and persistently
through all the moments
of our lives.
May we make
our relationship
with You complete
by choosing
to love You back.

Amen.

6

Sharing Jesus' Passion

Then the soldiers of the governor took Jesus into the governor's headquarters, and they gathered the whole cohort around him. They stripped him and put a scarlet robe on him, and after twisting some thorns into a crown, they put it on his head. They put a reed in his right hand and knelt before him and mocked him, saying, "Hail, King of the Jews!" They spat on him, and took the reed and struck him on the head. After mocking him, they stripped him of the robe and put his own clothes on him. Then they led him away to crucify him.

—*Matthew 27: 27-31*

Sometimes during our lives we go through trials that cause us to suffer physical, emotional, and spiritual pain. Suffering is part of being human. Often suffering is very unpleasant and we may try to avoid suffering at all costs. However, suffering plays an important part in our development as Christians and is of great value as we live in imitation of Christ. That is because suffering plays an important part in loving!

While the experience of love can be very pleasurable, love can also cause us great pain. For example, when someone we cherish dies, we experience profound sorrow. When we acknowledge the suffering of another person, empathize with them, and serve them, we share their pain. By having relationships with people we risk experiencing pain many different ways. Love can cost us much. His love for us cost Jesus everything.

To mature spiritually, we must understand how we feel about suffering. Then we can change how we react to trials if need be. Ask yourself these questions. Do you feel that suffering is worthless? Do you feel that suffering is a part of life that God can use in some way for greater good? Do you try to accept difficulties patiently while relying on God's strength to get you through? Are you willing to accept suffering if God is asking you to?

Those caring for the sick, young, frail, lonely, abandoned, and those in need are wonderful examples of sharing the same sacrificial love that Jesus shows to each of us. What we do to help those in need we also do for Jesus. On the other hand, when we allow ourselves to be the ones ministered to, we cooperate with the Christ-like service of other people. Let us take care not to block the actions of God working through others!

> Do you try to accept difficulties patiently while relying on God's strength to get you through?

Pain can cause us to sometimes pull away from what is or what we think is causing us pain. Sometimes while suffering we may blame God or distance ourselves from Him. However, suffering is of great value to us. Just as a sculptor carves his masterpiece to perfection over time and with much effort and attention, so too are we sculpted and refined as people through painful experiences. *"My brothers and sisters, whenever you face trials of any kind, consider it nothing but joy, because you know that the testing of your faith produces endurance; and let endurance have its full effect, so that you may be mature and complete, lacking in nothing"* (James 1:2-4).

By taking a look at how we act when we are frustrated, disappointed, when we have to wait, when we have lost or are separated from someone or something we care about, are led down an unexpected path, or when we are in pain, we gain important insight about how we view suffering. Do we become frustrated when events shock us out of our comfort zone or when we experience discomfort? Do we ask God that we and others get exactly what we want? Or do we pray for the strength to keep trying and remain faithful to God and His plans? Do we see our plans as being better than God's plans? Are we willing to wait, patiently and with trust, for events to play out according to God's plans if that is what He asks of us?

Some of the difficulties teenagers face include peer pressure, conflict with teachers, parents, and other kids, managing homework, illness, the loss of a loved one, changing schools, and moving. Sometimes terrible things happen. The goal is to trust God, especially when life is most difficult, and ask Him for help when we are suffering. May we see all circumstances as opportunities to bring us closer to God and to each other.

If we are unwilling to accept the discomfort and pain of trials, neither we nor our Christian discipleship can ever mature to become extraordinary. We increase our sanctity when we patiently cooperate with God

> The goal is to trust God, especially when life is most difficult, and ask Him for help when we are suffering.

through all circumstances. How often we have the misconception that God is very close during prosperity and is very distant during trials! Actually, God is never so close to us as when we accept difficulties with great love. Why? When we bear our trials patiently and lovingly, we resemble Jesus. Hardships teach us compassion and remind us that it is important to think about the needs of others. Often during trials we find God loving us through the compassion of others. Great things are accomplished when we persevere through trials and allow God to work in us and through us.

Just as Jesus' crucifixion led to our redemption and was followed by His glorious resurrection, so too can our suffering be followed by our own resurrection of sorts: closeness with God, personal growth, greater holiness, a deeper faith, and greater

> Many times we are able to serve others better and become more compassionate as a result of our trials.

compassion for others. The outcome is love! Something very critical happens during times of difficulty: We find ourselves more willing to turn to God. Whenever we suffer we should ask God, "What are You trying to tell/show/teach me?"

Suffering provides us the opportunity to reevaluate, learn, and grow in virtue and love. Suffering is essential to our life's work. Many times we are able to serve others better and become more compassionate as a result of our trials. How important it is to be open to God's plan during such pivotal times, and maintain our trust in Him.

Certainly the suffering Jesus endured throughout His lifetime and at the time of His death had great purpose. As discussed in Chapter 2, Jesus suffered a great deal during His mortal life. He embraced a life of poverty and service, living and dying for our sake. God chose to do this to help us. What would have happened if Jesus decided not to suffer for us? What happens when we resist during times of trial instead of being open to God's plans?

Jesus' personal ministry was one of sacrificial love. *"Now before the festival of the Passover, Jesus knew that his hour had come to depart from this world and go to the Father. Having loved his own who were in the world, he loved them to the end"* (John 13:1). Let us boldly define trials as events having tremendous value that extend beyond ourselves to benefit countless others. Let us examine the essential role of suffering in our personal apostolate by looking to Jesus as our model to imitate. "Every pain patiently borne, every blow to self, shapes the real eternal self. It was the Crucifixion of Our Lord that prepared the way for His Resurrection and Glory."[9]

In previous chapters we discussed acknowledging God's presence in our lives, accepting His love, loving Him in return, and allowing Him to use us as instruments of His love. This process can be refined and can come to fruition through suffering. Consider this beautiful description by Fulton J. Sheen, "Every tear, disappointment and grieved heart is a blank check. If we write our name on it, it is worthless. If we sign it with Christ's Name, it is infinite in its value. In prosperity, Christ gives you His gifts; in suffering with faith, He gives you Himself."[10]

> Let us boldly define trials as events having tremendous value that extend beyond ourselves to benefit countless others.

9 Fulton J. Sheen, *Our Grounds For Hope*, p. 36
10 Fulton J. Sheen, *Our Grounds For Hope*, p. 14

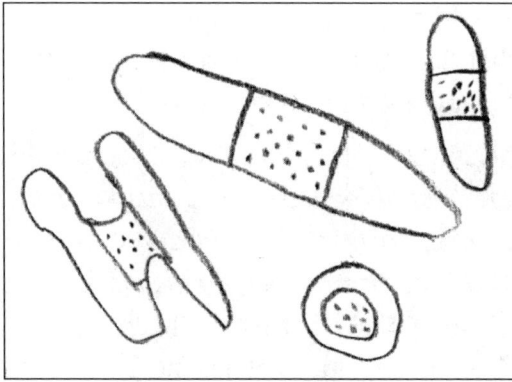

SHARING JESUS' PASSION
Uniting Our Injuries with Those of Jesus

Sometimes when I play outside in my yard I fall. I usually get up and continue playing, but sometimes I remain down because I am cut. Injuries can hurt really bad. Sometimes I have been hurt and could not make it back to the house. My family has always been there to help me up and give me pain reliever and comfort. The love of my family makes the pain seem to go away.

Receiving love and care helps me heal. Then I am able to get up and continue playing and having fun. I may remember the pain from an injury, but what stands out in my mind more than anything else is the comfort I received from my family. One cut can really hurt a lot, but imagine having thousands and thousands of them everywhere. That would be unbearable! Imagine enduring such pain for someone you love. Jesus endured such tremendous suffering because of his immeasurable love for each of us.

Consider the great suffering we feel when we have one cut or bruise on our bodies. Well, what about Jesus? If one cut hurts us so bad then how did He feel? He was on the brink of death carrying His Cross and knew that when He was done carrying His Cross to Calvary they were going to crucify Him. What was His motivation to keep going?

Jesus' motivation was not to die on the Cross for nothing. His motivation was to die on the Cross for us. His great love for us is what kept Him going. He died to save us from our sins so that we may someday go to heaven and be with Him forever. That motivation was in His mind.

Jesus also had loved ones there to encourage Him. His mother was there suffering along with Him, and His beloved Apostle John was there also. They were there to embrace Jesus, just like my family embraces me when I am hurt. His family was there to the very end for Him. Jesus gave John a special privilege. John was given the privilege of being a son to Mary after Jesus died. Jesus also gave each of us Mary as our Mother. So just like the Blessed Mother and John, we must stick by Jesus to the very end and we will be rewarded one day by our Father in heaven.

SHARING JESUS' PASSION
Questions for You

+ In what ways have your trials helped you to grow closer to God and to others?

+ Have you asked for God's guidance and for patience during suffering?

+ Do you ask for the grace to see events from His perspective?

+ Do you feel greater love for Jesus knowing He chose to suffer for your sake?

+ How has suffering affected your developing apostolate?

Dear God,

Please grant us the grace
to trust in You always,
and to view trials as opportunities
to grow closer to You and to others.
Guide us
as we open our hearts
and allow ourselves
to develop
and be transformed
into the likeness
of Your Son Jesus.

Amen.

7

His Resurrection and Our Journey

While they were talking about this, Jesus himself stood among them and said to them, "Peace be with you." They were startled and terrified, and thought that they were seeing a ghost. He said to them, "Why are you frightened, and why do doubts arise in your hearts? Look at my hands and my feet; see that it is I myself. Touch me and see; for a ghost does not have flesh and bones as you see that I have." And when he had said this, he showed them his hands and his feet. While in their joy they were disbelieving and still wondering, he said to them, "Have you anything here to eat?" They gave him a piece of broiled fish, and he took it and ate in their presence. Then he said to them, "These are my words that I spoke to you while I was still with you—that everything written about me in the law of Moses, the prophets, and the psalms must be fulfilled." Then he opened their minds to understand the scriptures, and he said to them, "Thus it is written, that the Messiah is to suffer and to rise from the dead on the third day, and that repentance and forgiveness of sins is to be proclaimed in his name to all nations, beginning from Jerusalem."

—Luke 24:36-47

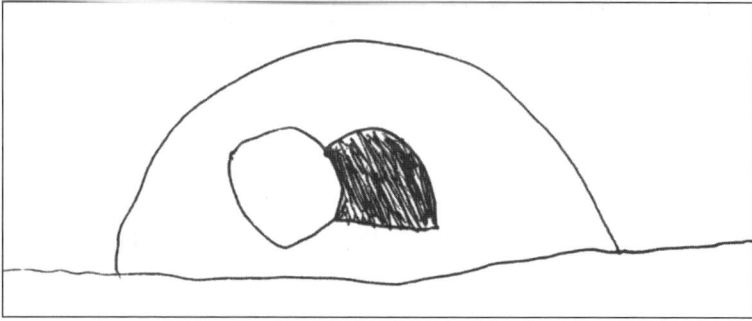

Imagine what life was like for Mary, the Apostles, and the followers of Jesus immediately after His passion and death. They must have felt stunned and terribly sad. Perhaps they also felt confused and uncertain like they did in Jesus' final days: *"They went on from there and passed through Galilee. He did not want anyone to know it; for he was teaching his disciples, saying to them, 'The Son of Man is to be betrayed into human hands, and they will kill him, and three days after being killed, he will rise again.' But they did not understand what he was saying and were afraid to ask him"* (Mark 9:30-32).

God's plan did not end when Jesus died because on the third day He resurrected as foretold in the Old Testament. Imagine the joy His beloved Mother, Apostles, and followers experienced when Jesus appeared to them! *"Now the eleven disciples went to Galilee, to the mountain to which Jesus had directed them. When they saw Him, they worshiped Him; but some doubted. And Jesus came and said to them, "All authority in heaven and on earth has been given to me. Go therefore and make disciples of all nations, baptizing them in the name of the Father and of the Son and of the Holy Spirit, and teaching them to obey everything that I have commanded you. And remember, I am with you always, to the end of the age"* (Matthew 28:16-20).

Jesus' Mother and His Apostles and followers experienced dramatic changes to their apostolic life after His death and resurrection. They accepted God's role for them in His plan of salvation, and the Catholic Church spread throughout the world. The previous chapter covered the important role suffering plays in our relationship with God and in our service to one another. We also considered how suffering can transform us as followers of Christ. Trials can motivate us to consider taking a path that we may never have considered otherwise, one that is more in conformity with God's Will.

> Fear and pain that are not resolved can handicap us.

Imagine if God came right out and said to several of the Apostles, "In three years I want you to stop fishing. The work you have done most of your life is about to change. After Jesus' crucifixion I will institute a new religion called Catholicism and you are going to travel extensively to bring it to people all over the world." What would their reaction have been? Instead, Jesus prepared His followers for their evolving apostolate throughout His public ministry and also after His death. The Holy Spirit enlightened them during Pentecost, and God continued to guide them through the Holy Spirit and Mary. Similarly, God prepares and guides each of us with His loving "Triune approach" through Mary, His Mother.

While trials may lead us to look outside our limited view so we can consider God's plan for us in a way we may not have thought about otherwise, difficulties can also lead us to behave in ways we would not otherwise. Fear and pain that are not resolved can handicap us. In the Bible passage quoted at the start of this chapter, Jesus acknowledged the feelings of

His Mother and the Apostles when He appeared to them after His resurrection. He stated "Why are you frightened, and why do doubts arise in your hearts?" Jesus reassured and instructed them, stating that as it was foretold, He would suffer and rise again on the third day, and repentance and forgiveness of sins should be preached to all nations in His name.

Great good came out of Jesus' sacrifice for us, and His presence after the Resurrection must have brought His loved ones great comfort. Jesus did not tell anyone to get even, to hold a grudge, or remain in despair. God had work for them to accomplish! He wants us to ask Him for healing and also allow ourselves to be forgiven while forgiving others so we can best share in His great ministry of love. God is always ready and available to heal us, so ask God to mend your wounds and He will.

> Jesus did not tell anyone to get even, to hold a grudge, or remain in despair. God had work for them to accomplish!

Earlier in this book it was mentioned that once we have made the decision to have a relationship, that relationship needs to be nurtured. Our relationship with God can have its ups and downs just like our relationships with people do. We have the security of knowing that God always remains the same and loves us unconditionally. We can be especially tempted to doubt when we suffer. Sometimes even though we love God we decide to hold back from greater faith, intimacy, and trust. This can happen when we are disappointed or hurt. Perhaps we have been hurt by our own choices, or we have been hurt by people and events in our lives. Unresolved anger, grief, and trauma can cause us to resist when things do not work out the way we had hoped or planned.

Throughout life we need to ask God to help us recognize what our hurts are. The God who created us understands exactly how we feel and why we feel the way we do. He patiently waits for us to accept all He has to offer us. Each person has been given a unique mission in conjunction with God's divine plan. Each of us has our own unique talents and we are always learning. Even if our gifts are not always known to us, each of us has them and each of us is necessary. **The world benefits from the contributions of every person's Christian service, including yours.**

"The reason moments of catastrophe may be the eves of spiritual victory is because it is in those moments of defeat that man's pride is most humbled and his soul thus prepared for the help of God....It is only when Peter had labored all the night and taken nothing that he was given the miraculous draught of fishes."[11] Tests prepare us for growth and change. Ask God to reveal to you how He wants you to serve Him throughout your evolving apostolate.

When we ask God to guide us in our efforts, He will! Do not doubt, for the God who can make something out of absolutely nothing can provide for our needs. He longs to bring us peace, healing, and inspiration when we are ready. The first step is to make the decision to acknowledge God and accept Him into our lives. Then we must put forth the effort to have our relationship with Him grow. Like the Good Thief, our reward will be great.

---

11 Fulton J. Sheen, *Our Grounds For Hope*, p. 31-32

HIS RESURRECTION AND OUR JOURNEY
Beauty at the Dunes

One of my favorite places to visit is the Sleeping Bear National Lakeshore in western Michigan. My family has a favorite trail that begins in the small town of Empire. The path is 1½ miles long and winds up and down through old farm orchards, fields, and forests. At the end of the trail is a scenic overlook with breathtaking views of Lake Michigan and the incredible sand dunes.

Most of the trail goes through the woods, but some of it is sandy and goes up a mountain where one can stand and see miles out into the lake. Years ago when I was smaller we took the trail all the way to the end, but we could not see beyond several feet in front of us because of the extremely thick fog. We knew there was a huge drop-off in front of us, but we could not see it or the lake!

This summer we returned to Empire and took the 1½-mile trail to the bluff by the lake. There was no fog this time and we finally got a chance to see the spectacular view we had missed before. The water was many different colors. The clouds cast shadows on the sand dunes and constantly changed the colors and the hues of the view. I am glad I was old enough to see the view clearly and remember it.

We can think about my two trips when my family walked on the trail in terms of Jesus' death and His resurrection. During His passion and death, things seemed foggy to His followers. They did not understand completely what was happening, and why the most loving of men had to undergo such mistreatment and be put to death. They were very traumatized by how Jesus was mistreated. Things must have been very unclear. Perhaps they asked themselves, like we sometimes do, "How can this be part of God's plan?" After Jesus' resurrection things became clearer, like my view of the lake on that sunny day. Whether things are foggy or clear to us, God is always present, just like the beautiful lake was there even when we could not see it.

HIS RESURRECTION AND OUR JOURNEY
Questions for You

+ Have you ever become angry with God or blamed Him during trials?

+ How long did God patiently wait for you to accept His encouragement and strength?

+ What helped you to get through difficulties?

+ Do you feel that suffering provides an opportunity to grow spiritually and personally?

+ How has your personal apostolate evolved over time?

Dear God,

May we find
personal strength and healing
in the example of
Your glorious resurrection.
Help us to persevere beyond trials
to find joy and purpose
as we serve You
through our dynamic and evolving
personal apostolate.

Amen.

The Crucial Role of Sanctity

8

> *Jesus went out again beside the sea; the whole crowd gathered around him, and he taught them. As he was walking along, he saw Levi, son of Alphaeus, sitting at the tax booth, and he said to him, "Follow me." And he got up and followed him. And as he sat at dinner in Levi's house, many tax collectors and sinners were also sitting with Jesus and his disciples – for there were many who followed him. When the scribes of the Pharisees saw that he was eating with sinners and tax collectors, they said to his disciples, "Why does he eat with tax collectors and sinners?" When Jesus heard this, he said to them, "Those who are well have no need of a physician, but those who are sick; I have come to call not the righteous but sinners."*
> —Mark 2:13-17

Jesus' decision to eat with tax collectors and sinners was shocking behavior in those times. Nevertheless, Jesus sought out sinners throughout His public ministry. The Pharisees were very angry that He lived among, taught, and reached out to sinners. Jesus continues this "shocking" behavior in our time as He lovingly reaches out to us. Loving us is never scandalous behavior to God, and yet we still sometimes resist when He challenges us to be holy and happy.

This chapter discusses how important it is to make holy choices day by day, moment by moment, as we serve God through our apostolate. When Adam and Eve committed the first sin, God's original plan for us was changed by that sin, which led to a division between man and God. Yet God continued to love us and promised to send a Savior who would conquer sin and restore the human race. At the appointed time, Jesus became Man and took our sins upon Himself to satisfy divine justice. The fulfillment of God's plan came about through the sacrificial love and obedience of Jesus.

Jesus' passion and death on the Cross made it possible for all people to go to heaven. However, to make God's plan come to fruition, each of us must cooperate in our own salvation. Even though Jesus died to save us, sin continues to distance each one of us from God and a soul can still perish of its own free will by deciding not to cooperate with Him. "God wants us 'all to be saved'; for this reason He gave us His Son, and with Him and through Him, all the means necessary for our salvation. Therefore, if a soul is not saved, it alone will be responsible."[12]

Sanctity is "...the perfection of the Christian life.... As grace grows and flourishes in our soul, its influence becomes deeper and wider; and when this influence extends effectively to all our actions, directing them solely to God's glory and uniting us wholly to Him by means of charity, then we have reached the fullness of Christian life, sanctity."[13] *"As God's chosen ones, holy and beloved, clothe yourselves with compassion, kindness, humility, meekness, and patience. Bear with one another and, if anyone has a complaint against another, forgive each other; just as the Lord has forgiven you, so you also must forgive. Above all, clothe yourselves with love, which binds everything together in perfect harmony. And let the peace of Christ rule in your hearts, to which indeed you were called in the one body. And be thankful"* (Colossians 3:12-15).

> Our behavior leads to very real outcomes for ourselves and others.

Our salvation depends on our efforts to live holy lives. We can also help others be more holy by setting a good example. *"Be perfect, therefore, as your heavenly Father is perfect"* (Matthew 5:48). To make our salvation possible, we must cooperate with God in the choices we make. Our behavior leads

---

12 Father Gabriel of St. Mary Magdalen, O.C.D., *Divine Intimacy* p. 6

13 Father Gabriel of St. Mary Magdalen, O.C.D., *Divine Intimacy* p. 9

to very real outcomes for ourselves and others. Sanctity is necessary to discipleship as we try our best to live holy lives and encourage holiness in others. To live in uniformity with God's will, we must make being holy a way of life. *"If you love me, you will keep my commandments"* (John 14:15).

When does sanctity begin within us? "Baptism has deposited within us this seed of sanctity, which is grace, a seed capable of blossoming into precious fruits of supernatural and eternal life for the soul that zealously cultivates it. By elevating us to the supernatural state, grace makes us capable of entering into relations with the Blessed Trinity, that is, capable of knowing and loving God as He is in Himself, as He knows and loves Himself."[14]

To grow in sanctity, we must live and love heroically. This is accomplished when we follow God's commandments. We become sanctified when we honor His Sacraments, go to Mass as often as we can, make frequent use of the Sacrament of Reconciliation, and do penance for our sins. We become like Jesus when we receive Him in the Eucharist. We become more Christ-like when we talk to God in prayer, read His Living Word in the Bible, and learn about our Catholic faith.

> An important part of living a holy life is to share God's love however and whenever we can with other people.

We become holy when we are obedient to His Will. "Our following of Christ, who is God made man, is the infallible road to sanctity. This same incarnate God is the source of all the

---

14 Father Gabriel of St. Mary Magdalen, O.C.D., *Divine Intimacy,* p. 9.

graces we need to become holy. As He told us, 'Without me you can do nothing.' Without His grace, our minds are blind. Without His grace, our wills are helpless to do what He wants of us to reach that blessed destiny for which we were made."[15]

An important part of living a holy life is to share God's love however and whenever we can with other people. "It has been said it makes no difference what you believe; it all depends on how you act. This is psychological nonsense, for a man acts out of his beliefs. Our Lord placed truth or belief in Him first; then came sanctification and good deeds. But here truth was not a vague ideal, but a Person. Truth was now lovable, because only a Person is lovable. Sanctity becomes the response the heart makes to Divine truth and its unlimited mercy to humanity."[16]

"Beloved, let us love one another, because love is from God; everyone who loves is born of God and knows God. Whoever does not love does not know God, for God is love. God's love was revealed among us in this way: God sent his only Son into the world so that we might live through him. In this is love, not that we loved God but that he loved us and sent his Son to be the atoning sacrifice for our sins. Beloved, since God loved us so much, we also ought to love one another. No one has ever seen God; if we love one another, God lives in us, and his love is perfected in us" (1 John 4:7-12).

Sanctity is crucial to loving God, ourselves, and each other and is essential to our apostolate. Each of us is called to live a holy life. **We are called to be saints!** We become sanctified through the effort we put into our relationship with God, and our sanctity bears much fruit through our apostolate. May we look to God to strengthen and guide us as we grow in holiness, each and every day.

---

15 Father John A. Hardon, S.J. Archives, *Christology*

16 Fulton J. Sheen, *Life of Christ*, p. 313

THE CRUCIAL ROLE OF SANCTITY
Participating in the Mass

I have been an altar server at my church since 4th grade. In our parish, there are four altar servers at every Mass with three different jobs to do. Two altar servers each carry a candle during the procession to the altar at the start of Mass and also hold a candle during the Gospel reading. One person carries the Cross down the main isle during the opening procession and back up again at the end of Mass. A fourth person holds the Bible for the priest during prayers. The people who carry the Cross and hold the Bible also have several other jobs to do during the Mass, including bringing the priest holy water and a towel before the Consecration.

The easiest job to remember is being a candle holder. I usually get the candle position because I get to the church early and choose the job I prefer. I usually altar serve with my brother Nick. Sometimes it is hard to remember what responsibilities go along with holding the Bible or carrying the Cross. It would be easier to sit in the pew and not altar serve, but altar serving gives me a different perspective and helps me concentrate on the Mass. Altar servers sit up front, get to see what is happening, and participate in the Mass. Anyone who assists during Mass obtains graces. I contribute to the Mass when I altar serve.

There are other ways to contribute during Mass, including welcoming people, lectoring, bringing down the gifts, playing music, being a Mass coordinator, ushering, running the slides, being an Extraordinary Minister of Holy Communion, or being a cantor. We all participate in the Mass when we pray out loud, sing, greet each other, and receive the Eucharist as a community. Participating can be as simple as smiling at your neighbor in the pew. Without the contributions of each person, the Mass would not be the same. Participating and contributing during Mass is part of everyone's apostolate.

Sometimes God asks us to step out of our comfort zone and do something new or different. When we cooperate with his promptings, we find out that we may like something that perhaps we did not consider before. We grow as individuals. Our apostolate evolves this way and we become sanctified. Sometimes being holy is the hardest option when we have a choice to make. Living in imitation of Christ is not always easy but the rewards are eternal.

THE CRUCIAL ROLE OF SANCTITY
Questions for You

+ In what ways are you taking responsibility for your salvation by living a holy life?

+ What are some other ways you can increase your sanctity?

+ Do you see your life as having great purpose?

+ Are you embracing that purpose fully?

+ Have you asked God to help you?

> Dear God,
>
> Please help us to embrace
> Your magnificent offer
> of redemption and sanctification,
> made possible and obtainable by
> the power of
> Your great love for each of us.
> May we strive to help others
> in this mission we all share
> through the loving service
> of our apostolate.
>
> Amen.

9

The Greatest Commandment

Now before the festival of the Passover, Jesus knew that his hour had come to depart from this world and go to the Father. Having loved his own who were in the world, he loved them to the end....And during supper Jesus, knowing that the Father had given all things into his hands, and that he had come from God and was going to God, got up from the table, took off his outer robe, and tied a towel around himself. Then he poured water into a basin and began to wash the disciples' feet and to wipe them with the towel that was tied around him. He came to Simon Peter, who said to him, "Lord, are you going to wash my feet?" Jesus answered, "You do not know now what I am doing, but later you will understand." Peter said to him, "You will never wash my feet." Jesus answered, "Unless I wash you, you have no share with me." —John 13:2-8

After he had washed their feet, had put on his robe, and had returned to the table, he said to them, "Do you know what I have done to you? You call me Teacher and Lord—and you are right, for that is what I am. So if I, your Lord and Teacher, have washed your feet, you also ought to wash one another's feet. For I have set you an example, that you also should do as I have done to you."

—John 13:12-15

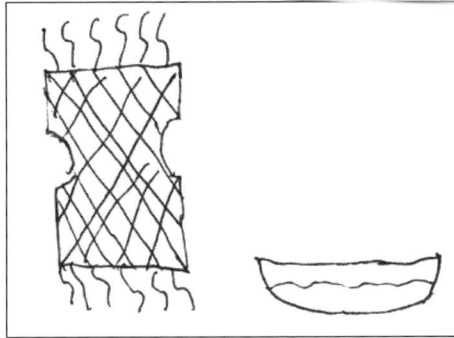

Imagine in your mind what the scene was like as Jesus, a member of the Blessed Trinity, laid aside His garments, wrapped a towel around His waist, and washed the feet of His Apostles. Our Master became the servant as He lovingly placed Himself at the service of all humanity. Once again, Jesus' action opposed the customs of that time. Peter realized this, and stated, "Lord, are you going to wash my feet?…You will never wash my feet."

Jesus would have it otherwise, and very clearly instructed everyone through all time with His words, "So if I, your Lord and Teacher, have washed your feet, you also ought to wash one another's feet. For I have set you an example, that you also should do as I have done to you." Jesus consistently served others throughout His life. He came to redeem and sanctify, and role-modeled the proper etiquette God desires of all people, regardless of our era, race, culture, or social standing.

"Do nothing from selfish ambition or conceit, but in humility regard others as better than yourselves. Let each of you look not to your own interests, but to the interests of others. Let the same mind be in you that was in Christ Jesus, who, though he was in the form of God, did not regard equality

with God as something to be exploited, but emptied himself, taking the form of a slave, being born in human likeness. And being found in human form, he humbled himself and became obedient to the point of death—even death on a cross" (Philippians 2:3-8).

So far in this book we have discussed recognizing and acknowledging God's love for us. We highlighted the significant impact the apostolates of Jesus, Mary, and Joseph had and continue to have on all humanity. We look to them as examples to follow as we, too, unite our actions with the will of God. We examined the many ways God's love entices us

> **Each of us must acknowledge the contribution that every person makes through his or her own unique mission.**

to faith. We also discussed making the decision to accept God's love in the many ways His love is shown, and how He awaits our love in return. We discussed the role of suffering in our lives and how our sufferings and triumphs imitate Jesus' death and resurrection. Then we discussed the importance of living holy lives.

This closing chapter focuses on sharing God's love with others every day, moment by moment, through our personal apostolate. In this way we fulfill God's greatest commandment to love one another as He loves us. Multiple choices are brought together: acknowledging God's love, accepting His love, loving Him in return, and loving others. In order for our discipleship to truly follow the will of God, **each of us must acknowledge the contribution that every person makes**

through his or her own unique mission. To do so we must respect and defend every single person's right to life. *"You shall love the Lord your God with all your heart, and with all your soul, and with all your strength, and with all your mind; and your neighbor as yourself"* (Luke 10:27).

Every apostolate begins at the moment of conception. *"For it was you who formed my inward parts; you knit me together in my mother's womb. I praise you, for I am fearfully and wonderfully made. Wonderful are your works; that I know very well. My frame was not hidden from you, when I was being made in secret, intricately woven in the depths of the earth. Your eyes beheld my unformed substance. In your book were written all the days that were formed for me, when none of them as yet existed"* (Psalm 139: 13-16).

Before we were even born, each of us already began impacting the lives of others and contributing to their welfare. **So much good is accomplished by our very existence!** In general terms, each evolving apostolate is fulfilled through our roles as embryos, infants, children, adolescents, adults, and senior citizens. They include what we accomplish as students, patients, or retirees, while in training, through various occupations that are paid or unpaid, through volunteering, in sickness and in health. More specifically, our apostolate includes the many ways we serve God each and every day, from moment to moment.

> Before we were even born, each of us already began impacting the lives of others and contributing to their welfare.

While some of us love and serve

others through what we are able to do physically, our contributions are not limited to what can be seen by eyes, felt with hands, measured, heard, counted, or quoted. Our contributions may be tangible and have clearly visible results, or may be significant while remaining unseen. For example, people who are unable to care for themselves have great purpose and a vital apostolate, and we must give them every opportunity to share their gifts. They provide love in many ways and contribute greatly to society. Remarkable things are accomplished through their circumstances because they teach us compassion while fulfilling the will of God.

The effects of our apostolate do not have to be physically observable to be real. There are great contributions taking place all around us every day that cannot be seen. God's love is real. The effect He has on our lives is real. Just as real is His love resonating through the discipleship of each and every

> There are great contributions taking place all around us every day that cannot be seen.

person. In His encyclical *The Gospel of Life*, Pope John Paul II stated, "The blood of Christ, while it reveals the grandeur of the Father's love, *shows how precious man is in God's eyes and how priceless the value of his life.*"[17]

The Christ-likeness of St. Thérèse of Lisieux provides us with a very powerful example of the effects our lives have as followers of Christ when we choose to live and serve in love. St. Thérèse wrote in *Story of a Soul,* "Charity gave me the key to my vocation. I understood that if the Church

---

17 Pope John Paul II, *The Gospel of Life*, p. 45

had a body composed of different members, the most necessary and most noble of all could not be lacking to it, and so I understood that the church had a Heart and that this Heart was BURNING WITH LOVE. I understood it was Love alone that made the Church's members act...I understand that LOVE COMPRISED ALL VOCATIONS, THAT LOVE WAS EVERYTHING, THAT IT EMBRACED ALL TIMES AND PLACES...IN A WORD, THAT IT WAS ETERNAL!"[18] Her vocation, her personal apostolate, was love.

In conclusion, it is worth repeating: **You are very, very special to God**. Every single person ever created is special to God! He loves each of us immensely. Imagine how you felt during the happiest, most loving moment you have ever had. Multiply that feeling by the largest number you can think of, and you still will not even come close to how much God loves each one of us. At conception each person is gifted by God with striking uniqueness, individual talents, traits, personalities, and an apostolate that changes through life as we develop and as our circumstances change. For the sake of our sanctity and the work we accomplish in our imitation of Christ, each of us must recognize, respect, and protect the uniqueness and mutual importance of every other person's contribution as it was intended by God.

Everyone has something to contribute, for no one was ever created without a purpose. Through our apostolate we return our treasures of self to the infinitely loving God who gave them to us in the first place. We return love for love while serving Him and His people. Our presence, thoughts, desires, words and actions give witness to God's love in our world. May God bless you for your efforts on His behalf and may your life bring God, you, and others great joy.

---

18 St. Thérèse of Lisieux, *Story of a Soul*, p. 194

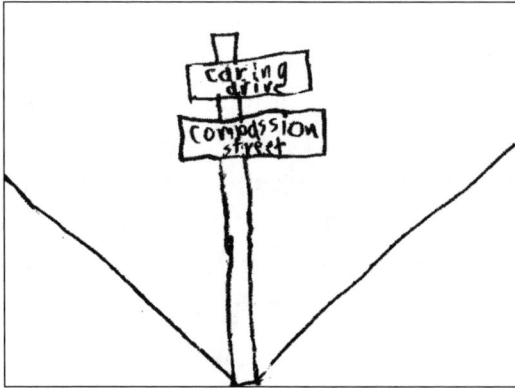

THE GREATEST COMMANDMENT:
Love Your Neighbor

My neighborhood is very beautiful and lively. Most of my neighbors like to decorate their yards with flowers. My family sees many people go by our house on walks with their dogs. We have a very nice neighbor across the street who is friends with my mom. Her son is friends with me, my brother, and my sister and we enjoy playing together. The neighbors that live behind us and the couple that lives next to them are very nice to us and give us flowers from their gardens. Some of our neighbors are grandparents and their grandchildren sometimes play with us when they visit.

We live on a corner so we have a second family living right across the street. That family has four girls. My sister enjoys inviting the younger two girls over to play. Sometimes they bring us treats, like homemade stained-glass candy at Christmas and strawberries and raspberry jam in the summer. One year they watered our flowers and garden while we were on vacation.

Two houses down from us lives a nice family with two children, one boy and one girl. They are a little younger than my sister. The children just got a little French bulldog puppy named Oliver and they sometimes bring him over to play with us. Another neighbor fixed our mailbox when it was hit by a car, and yet another neighbor fixed our mailbox after walking his dog and seeing that the hinge was broken.

We are so blessed to live among so many wonderful, caring people. We do kind things for our neighbors, too. We share flowers from our yard, send notes, entertain, collect mail, provide encouragement, watch children, and host games in our yard. Once we even rescued a pug that was wandering in the street. Last year we saw an injured skunk in our neighbor's yard and told her not to let her dog out. We try to be considerate of those around us and keep our yard looking nice. That includes keeping our bushes trimmed and adding flowers for color.

One family that lives close to us are nice people but they mow, edge, and blow grass clippings and leaves late at night and on holidays when other neighbors are entertaining or sitting out for a quiet evening. We all have our faults of course, but need to respect our neighbors because we share the same area. Without neighbors and friends around, we would be isolated and miss out on some wonderful opportunities to share God's love with one another.

We must always strive to be considerate. God told us to love our neighbor. That means loving not just our neighbors but everyone that we know like our friends, even our enemies, and those we come into contact with every single day. When we treat others with respect it pleases God, who asks that we love and serve others in His name.

THE GREATEST COMMANDMENT
A Question for You

+ How are you faithful to God's greatest commandments to love
  Him with all your heart and to love your neighbor as yourself?

Most Compassionate and Loving God,

Please bless us
as we seek to recognize
the many opportunities we have
to grow closer to You
and to each other
during the joys and sorrows
of our lives.
Help us to accept
Your loving offer
of salvation and sanctification,
and guide us as we
serve each other
on the journey toward heaven.

Amen.

Conclusion
The Story of Your Life

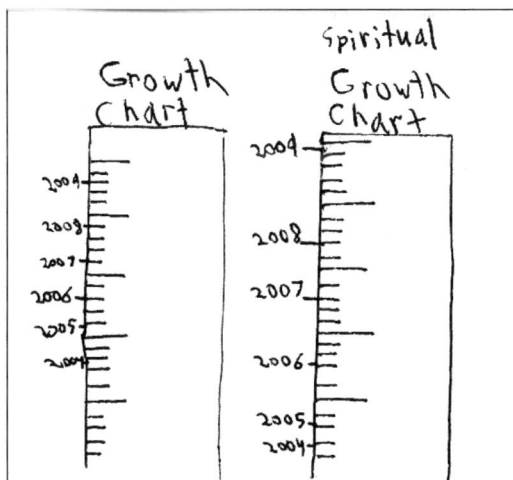

Growth Chart

Spiritual Growth Chart

O nce upon a time, God created wonderful, exciting, loving, valuable you. God created you for a reason: to know Him, love Him, and serve Him. *Your life has great purpose!* That purpose is revealed in the work of your apostolate.

Every person's apostolate is taking place at this very moment. Just as we do not stay the same through our lives, our life's work changes, too, as we make decisions based on what God asks of us. Jesus' apostolate evolved from growing in His mother's womb through His infancy, childhood, young adulthood, and adulthood. He lived His life privately until becoming well known during the three years of His public ministry. He was loved and persecuted, popular and unpopular, loved and hated, returned to Jerusalem a hero at the age of 33 and was crucified shortly after that. Several things remained the same through the different stages of Jesus' life: He was obedient to God and served others with great love.

Our imitation of Christ includes all we do during the different stages of our lives: as embryos, babies, children, teenagers, adults, and senior citizens. We serve Christ as students, whether we are employed, unemployed, stay-at-home, religious, whether we are in transition between jobs or careers, whether we are healthy or not, whether we are able bodied or disabled. Our apostolate takes place through all the events of our lives. Our efforts to grow in holiness and share the love of God with one another not only help each of us individually, but benefit so many other people, including people we may never meet! Father John A. Hardon, S.J., S.T.D. stated on his audiotape, *He Will Come Again to Judge the Living and the Dead*, "No human act is sterile. We are writing history for eternity."[19]

Just as we benefit from God's love in so many different ways, through so many different people, so too are we called through our apostolate to share God's love with others. So beautiful is His love that it will not be denied and can never be contained. God's love is extremely contagious! *"I am confident of this, that the one who began a good work among you will bring it to completion by the day of Jesus Christ"* (Philippians 1:6). Imagine the moment when you will one day stand before God and share with Him the many ways you loved Him back throughout your life, directly and by serving in His place. How beautiful that moment will be!

The beginning.

---

19 Rev. John A. Hardon, S.J., S.T.D., *He Will Come Again to Judge the Living and the Dead*, audiotape.

Your Teen Apostolate:
Accepting and Sharing the Love of God
Questions for Individual or Group Discussion

1 **We Are Loved** + In what ways do you recognize God's great love for you?

2 **Following the Holy Family** + How do the lives of Jesus, Mary, and Joseph inspire you in your own life?

3 **Called to Faith** + What are three things that have led you to believe and trust in God?

4 **Accepting God's Love** + What are some of the ways that you accept God's love?

5 **Loving God Back** + How do you love God in return?

6 **Sharing Jesus' Passion** + Has suffering affected your service to God and others? How so?

7 **His Resurrection and Our Journey** + What has happened in your own life that helps you relate to Jesus' resurrection?

8 **The Crucial Role of Sanctity** + What are some things that you can do to become more holy?

9 **The Greatest Commandment** + How do you follow God's greatest commandments to love Him with all your heart, with all your soul, and with all your mind, and to love your neighbor as yourself?

Acknowledgements

I thank God for inspiring me, and my mom for encouraging me to write this book for teenagers. I am grateful for my family and my two ferrets, Cupcake and Lily. I would like to thank you for taking the time to read this book, and hope that your faith and love for God grows. I would also like to thank all those who have encouraged me and supported me, especially my brother Nick and sister Alyssa. I thank my Oma and Aunt Belinda for always being there for me and caring for me. I would like to thank Andrea Dabrowski for being a great friend and for writing the foreword to this book. Lastly, I thank Van and Linda and the staff at South Street Skatepark in Rochester for their kindness and for allowing us to photograph at their facility.

—Andre Joseph Bottesi

My dear Lord, I thank you for the opportunity to love you and serve You through the power of the written word, and pray that this work is pleasing in Your sight. *Vulnera tua merita mea.* I am very grateful to my publishing "dream team," including editor and printer Erin Howarth at Wilderness Adventure Books, graphic designer Roseann Nieman at Niemanart Graphics, and photographer Kathy Rizzo. You are incredibly talented and delightful to work with.

I also thank my daughter Alyssa and son Nick who lent their support and ideas to this work. Thank you Andre, for being a wonderful collaborator in this labor of love for all those your age. You are very compassionate and have terrific ideas. May all teenagers come to realize in greater measure how much they are loved and valued, and understand the immense contribution they make to our world.

God is at work in all of you!

—Michele Elena Bondi

*I thank my God
every time I remember you.*
—Philippians 1:3

Sources and References

The Old and New Testament verses referenced throughout this book are quoted from *The Holy Bible: New Revised Standard Version* (Division of Christian Education of the National Council of Council of Churches of Christ in the United States of America, 1989).

PREFACE

1. "God has no need..." St. Thérèse of Lisieux, *Story of a Soul* (Washington, D.C.: ICS Publications, 1996).

1 WE ARE LOVED

2. "If you live for Christ..." Fulton J. Sheen, *Our Grounds for Hope* (Totowa, New Jersey: Catholic Book Publishing Co., 2000).

2 FOLLOWING THE HOLY FAMILY

3. "Mary's greatness consists in the fact…" Pope Benedict XVI, Encyclical *Letier Deus Caritas Est* (Rome: Libreria Editrice Vaticana, 2005).

4. "…He now sensed guilt to such an extent…" Fulton J. Sheen, *Life of Christ* (Garden City, New York: Doubleday, 1977).

4 ACCEPTING GOD'S LOVE

5. "The Gospel of Luke shows Jesus continually exercising His ministry of pardon" Ed. Raymond E. Brown, S.S.; Joseph A. Fitzmyer, S.J.; Roland E. Murphy, O. Carm., *The Jerome Biblical Commentary Vol. II: 44* (Englewood Cliffs, New Jersey: Prentice-Hall, 1968).

5 LOVING GOD BACK

6. "…love is repaid by love alone…" St. Thérèse of Lisieux, *Story of a Soul* (Washington, D.C.: ICS Publications, 1996).

7. "See, then, all that Jesus lays claim to from us…" St. Thérèse of Lisieux, *Story of a Soul* (Washington, D.C.: ICS Publications, 1996).

8. "If Jesus Christ thirsted for souls…" Fulton J. Sheen, *The Rainbow of Sorrow* (New York: Garden City Books, 1938).

6 SHARING JESUS' PASSION

9. "Every pain patiently borne, every blow to self…" Fulton J. Sheen, *Our Grounds for Hope* (Totowa, New Jersey: Catholic Book Publishing Company, 2000).

10. "Every tear, disappointment and grieved heart is a blank check…" Fulton J. Sheen, *Our Grounds for Hope* (Totowa, New Jersey: Catholic Book Publishing Company, 2000).

7 HIS RESURRECTION AND OUR JOURNEY

11. "The reason moments of catastrophe may be the eves of spiritual victory…" Fulton J. Sheen, *Our Grounds for Hope* (Totowa, New Jersey: Catholic Book Publishing Company, 2000).

8 THE CRUCIAL ROLE OF SANCTITY

12. "God wants us 'all to be saved'" Father Gabriel of St. Mary Magdalen, O.C.D., *Divine Intimacy* (Rockford, Illinois: Tan Publishers, 1996).

13. "…the perfection of the Christian life…" Father Gabriel of St. Mary Magdalen, O.C.D., *Divine Intimacy* (Rockford, Illinois: Tan Publishers, 1996).

14. "Baptism has deposited within us this seed of sanctity…" Father Gabriel of St. Mary Magdalen, O.C.D., *Divine Intimacy* (Rockford, Illinois: Tan Publishers, 1996).

15. "…our following of Christ, who is God made man…" *Christology*, Father John A. Hardon, S.J. Archives, Inter Merifica, www.therealpresence.org/archives, 1997 (accessed March 31, 2008).

16. "It has been said it makes no difference…" Fulton J. Sheen, *Life of Christ* (New York: Image Books, 1977).

9 THE GREATEST COMMANDMENT

17. "The blood of Christ…" Pope John Paul II, *The Gospel of Life* (New York: Random House, 1995).

18. "Charity gave me the key to my vocation…" St. Thérèse of Lisieux, *Story of a Soul* (Washington, D.C.: ICS Publications, 1996).

CONCLUSION

19. "No human act is sterile…" Rev. John A. Hardon, S.J., S.T.D., *He Will Come Again to Judge the Living and the Dead* (Bardstown, Kentucky: Eternal Life), audiotape.